Collins

easy learning

Grammar and punctuation

Ages 5–7

1 duck

3 ducks

How to use this book

- Find a quiet, comfortable place to work, away from other distractions.
- Tackle one topic at a time.
- Help with reading the instructions where necessary and ensure your child understands what to do.
- Encourage your child to check their own answers as they complete each activity.

- Discuss your child what they have learnt.
- Let your child return to their favourite pages once they have been completed, to talk about the activities.
- Reward your child with plenty of praise and encouragement.

Special features

- Yellow boxes: Introduce a topic and outline the key grammar or punctuation ideas.
- Red boxes: Emphasise a rule relating to the unit.
- Orange shaded boxes: Offer advice to parents on how to consolidate your child's understanding.

Useful definitions

Grammar	
Noun	A noun is a naming word, e.g. house, dog, kite
Proper noun	A noun that is the name of something particular, like a person, a day, a month or a place, e.g. Dan, Tuesday, June, India.
Verb	A verb is usually a doing word, e.g. run, jump, write. It tells you what is happening.
Singular	Singular means one.
Plural	Plural means more than one.
Adjective	An adjective is a word that describes a noun, e.g. green, big, cold.
Adverb	An adverb is a word that describes a verb (an action), e.g. quickly, carefully, angrily.
Punctuation	
Full stop	A full stop (.) shows where a sentence ends.
Question mark	A question mark (?) is used at the end of a sentence to show a question has been asked.
Comma	Commas have different uses. In this book they are used to separate items in a list.
Exclamation mark	An exclamation mark (!) is used at the end of a sentence to show shock, surprise, upset or a command.

Published by Collins
An imprint of HarperCollins*Publishers*
1 London Bridge Street
London SE1 9GF

Browse the complete Collins catalogue at
www.collins.co.uk

© HarperCollins*Publishers* 2012
This edition © HarperCollins*Publishers* 2015

10 9 8 7 6 5 4 3 2 1

ISBN 978-0-00-813432-7

The author and publisher are grateful to the copyright holders for permission to use the quoted materials and images.

p18 © kotyache/shutterstock.com;
p24 © Lorelyn Medina/shutterstock.com;
p25 © MrGarry/shutterstock.com

All rights reserved. No part of this publication may be reproduced, stored in a retrieval system, or transmitted, in any form or by any means, electronic, mechanical, photocopying, recording or otherwise, without the prior permission of Collins.

British Library Cataloguing in Publication Data

A Catalogue record for this publication is available from the British Library

Contributor: Rachel Grant
Page layout by Linda Miles, Lodestone Publishing and Contentra Technologies
Illustrated by Kathy Baxendale, Rachel Annie Bridgen, Graham Smith and Andy Tudor
Cover design by Sarah Duxbury and Paul Oates
Cover illustration by Kathy Baxendale
Project managed by Chantal Peacock and Sonia Dawkins

Contents

Capital letters

Capital letters:

A B C D E F G H I J K L M
N O P Q R S T U V W X Y Z

Every **sentence** starts with a capital letter.

The cat is asleep.

1 Add the missing capital letters.

A B ___ D E F ___ H I J K ___ M

N O ___ Q R ___ T U V W ___ Y Z

2 Copy the sentences.
Add the missing capital letters.

it is a hot day.

_____

the dog sat on a cat.

_____

we like sweets.

_____

Find examples to show your child that, as well as proper nouns, the personal pronoun 'I' is always a capital letter too.

Full stops

Most sentences end with a **full stop**.

The baby is crying.

1 Copy the sentences.
Add the missing full stops.

The pool is fun

_____

A girl plays tennis

_____

Dan walks to school

_____

The hen laid an egg

_____

2 Use your own words to finish the sentences.
Remember the full stop.

The cow eats _____

The dog barks _____

The baby smiles _____

Explain to your child that full stops give a signal to the reader that a pause is needed. Read a short text extract without pausing to illustrate the role of the full stops.

Nouns

Nouns are naming words.

gate   flower   grass

1 Use the nouns in the box to label the pictures.

> chair   dog   boat   sun   tree   ring

_____   _____   _____

_____   _____   _____

2 Look around you and list the nouns you can see.

How many have you listed?   **5** = good   **7** = great   **10** = fantastic

Ask your child to look around the room they are sitting in – list as many nouns as they can find.

Proper nouns 1

A **proper noun** is a noun that is the name of a person or place.

> **Proper nouns** always start with a capital letter.

Sam lives in **Spain**.

Amy lives in **Australia**.

1 Circle the proper nouns.

kite   **Meena**   **London**   man   **Ben**   **torch**   Africa

Cinderella   Tonkin Road   **coat**   **pen**   **Mr Atkin**   France

2 Answer the questions using a proper noun.
Remember the capital letters.

What is your name? _____

Which town do you live near? _____

Who is your best friend? _____

Who is your teacher? _____

Where did you go on holiday? _____

What is the name of your road? _____

Look in a reading book and ask your child to note the different proper nouns they can find. Introduce other proper nouns to your child, e.g. days, months, famous buildings or monuments.

Capital letters and full stops

Every sentence starts with a **capital letter**.
Most sentences end with a **full stop**.

The bird watches the fish**.**

1 Copy the sentences.
Add the missing capital letters and full stops.

it is raining

_____

we like playing games

_____

sam is swimming

_____

2 Use the words in the boxes to help you write your own sentences.

Friday   swimming   school

_____

lion   sleep   tree

_____

sweets   shop   buy

_____

Give your child further practice of **2** style questions, where they have to build their own sentences from given words.

Writing sentences 1

Words must be in the right order for **sentences** to make sense.

Grass sheep eat.   ✗
Sheep eat grass.   ✔

1 Tick the sentences that make sense.

The ice feels cold.　☐

The boy in stream.　☐

Dan forgot his book.　☐

The shop sells sweets.　☐

Ran as fast as he can.　☐

2 Write these words in the right order to make a sentence.

Anywhere sleep cats.

_____

Splash the puddles in children.

_____

Car grey is the.

_____

Write some short sentences for your child without capital letters and full stops. Ask them to rewrite them correctly.

Verbs

A **verb** is usually a doing word.
It tells us what is happening.

Max **runs** to the finish line.

1 Write the verb shown in each picture.

| skiing | cycling | eating | slipping | standing | laughing |

_____ _____ _____

_____ _____ _____

2 Choose five of the verbs in **1** and write them into sentences.

_____

_____

_____

_____

_____

_____

Verbs can be regular (walk, walked) or irregular (sing, sang). Although this topic doesn't cover this subject it is worth being aware of it in case your child notices that some verbs are different.

Questions

Questions help us find out things.

What is the time?

A question begins with a **capital letter** and ends with a **question mark**.

1 Copy and correctly write each question.

where are you going

_____

why is your coat muddy

_____

when can I eat my snack

_____

what is his name

_____

2 Write a question for each of these answers.

It is sunny and hot.

_____

You need to get up at 8 o'clock.

_____

My best friend is Rick.

_____

Discuss different types of questions with your child. Closed questions can be answered with a 'yes' or 'no'. Open questions have a variety of different answers.

Writing sentences 2

Sentences need to make sense.

Walks love dogs. ✘   Dogs love walks. ✔

1 The words in these sentences are mixed up.
Copy the words in the correct order to make each sentence.
Make sure you use capital letters and full stops.

feels   hot   the sun

_____

in the river   jumped   the dog

_____

ice cream   Keith   enjoys

_____

her bag   Anna   lost

_____

2 Use these words to write a sentence.
Remember the capital letter and the full stop.

holiday   we   going

_____

grumpy   teacher

_____

bites   lion   zookeeper

_____

Give your child a subject you know they find interesting, e.g. a pet. Ask them to write five sentences about the subject. Check it is punctuated properly.

Commas in lists

Commas are used in lists.

For lunch I've got crisps, a sandwich, an apple, chocolate and a drink.

Look carefully at where the commas are.

A comma is *not* needed where the word **and** is used.

1 Add the missing commas to the sentences.

In a car you find keys maps seats and seatbelts.

In a house you find doors windows beds tables and chairs.

In a wardrobe you find coats shirts trousers dresses and shoes.

In a shed you find pots seeds spades forks and rakes.

2 Sort the words in the box into lists.
(Hint: Some words may go into more than one list!)

> **floats   teachers   towels   stamps   packages   water
> goggles   books   displays   children   till   postmaster**

Things you find at a school:

_____

Things you find at a swimming pool:

_____

Things you find at a post office:

_____

Ask your child to write five sentences. In the first sentence ask them to use one comma, in the second sentence two commas and so on until they write a sentence with five commas.

Singular and plural

Nouns can be **singular** or **plural**.

Singular means *one*.

cat

Plural means *more than one*.

cat**s**

You add **s** to many singular nouns to make them plural.

If the singular noun ends in **sh**, **ch**, **ss** or **x**, you add **es** to make the plural noun.

church ⟶ church**es**

box ⟶ box**es**

Some singular nouns have different endings when you make the plural noun.

child ⟶ child**ren**

foot ⟶ **feet**

1 Fill in the missing singular and plural nouns.

spider _____

owl _____

_____ chips

man _____

_____ dishes

kiss _____

beach _____

Remind your child what a noun is. Ask them to look through their reading book in search of plural nouns. Can they find ten where an 's' is added? Can they find any which end in **es** or have different endings from those of the singular noun?

Proper nouns 2

Nouns are naming words.

Proper nouns are nouns that name something in particular, like a person, a place, a day or a month.

Jay went to **Magicland** on **Tuesday**.

Proper nouns always start with a capital letter.

1 Copy these sentences correctly.

We love walking barney on exmoor.

_____

alex roberts was late for school on monday.

_____

italy is further away than france.

_____

2 Copy this address correctly.

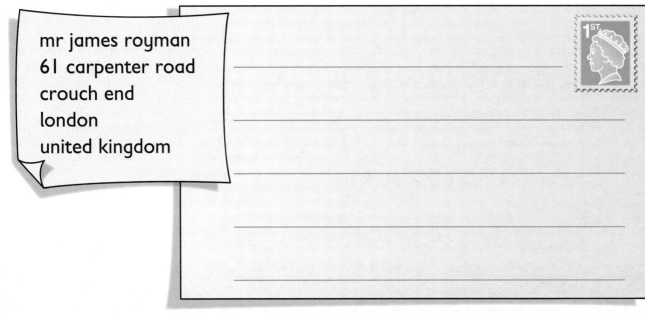

mr james royman
61 carpenter road
crouch end
london
united kingdom

How am I doing?

1 Sort these words into the table.
Remember the missing capital letters.

towel   **write**   kite   wales   **dance**   **lion**

run   cinderella   ben   kick   newspaper   thursday

Nouns	Proper nouns	Verbs

2 Write these sentences correctly.
Remember capital letters, full stops, commas and question marks.

march comes before april

_____

what time shall we meet

_____

don't forget to bring sweets crisps and apples

_____

can tom come to baker park too

_____

Look back at the topics that your child still finds tricky.

Joining sentences 1

Two short **sentences** can be joined by adding a word between them.

The lorry moved too fast. It knocked over a wall.
The lorry moved too fast **and** it knocked over a wall.
The men built a fence. The wind blew it over.
The men built a fence **but** the wind blew it over.

Short sentences can be joined with the words **and** or **but**.

1 Join the two short sentences with the words **and** or **but**.

The leaves fell off the tree. They were raked into a pile.

_____

Zack forgot his coat. He didn't forget his school bag.

_____

The bird caught a worm. It took the worm back to its nest.

_____

2 Finish the sentences in your own words.

Jane was tired **and** _____

The sun is out **but** _____

The mouse ran away from the cat **and** _____

_____

Ask your child to find examples of sentences joined with the words 'and' or 'but' in books at home.

Apostrophes 1

An apostrophe can show when a letter or letters have been missed out of a word. The apostrophe takes the place of the letter or letters that are missed out.

> This type of word is called a **contraction**.

I am = I'm   cannot = can't

I'm sorry I **can't** come to your party.

1. Write the contractions of these words. Use apostrophes where letters are missed out.

   has not _____

   they are _____

   could not _____

   I will _____

2. Copy the sentences. Add the missing apostrophes.

   Were having a great holiday.

   _____

   I cant wait to go swimming tonight.

   _____

   Lucy says shell be back soon.

   _____

   Harry didnt come to school today.

   _____

Give your child further contractions as shown in 1 and ask them to write sentences using them.

18

Adjectives

Adjectives are describing words.
They tell us more about **nouns**.

The hen laid **brown** eggs.
The hen laid **big** eggs.
The hen laid **two** eggs.

1 Circle the adjective in each sentence.

Ben walked home in the cold wind.

We had green beans for lunch.

France is a beautiful country.

Our grumpy cat scratched Fay's hand.

2 Use these adjectives in your own sentences.

lumpy

_____

loud

_____

funny

_____

tasty

_____

It helps children to realise there are different categories of adjectives, e.g. colour adjectives, number-order adjectives (e.g. third), shape adjectives, feelings adjectives, etc. Help your child to find some examples of adjectives in their reading book.

Joining sentences 2

Two short **sentences** can be joined by adding a word between them.

You can have juice. You can have water.
You can have juice **or** you can have water.

Short sentences can be joined with the words **and**, **but** or **or**.

When we use **or** as a connective we can shorten the sentence:

You can have juice **or** water.

The meaning is the same.

1 Use **and**, **but** or **or** to join these sentences.

The dog fell in the river. It couldn't get out.

_____

Did the cow slip on the ice? Did she slip in the mud?

_____

The red car is fast. The yellow car is faster.

_____

Dan worked hard on his sums. He still got them wrong.

_____

2 Finish the sentences in your own words.

Henry hurt himself **but** _____

We could go out tomorrow **or** _____

Matt worked hard **and** _____

Sentences can be joined with a number of different words. See if your child can find examples of different joining words in their reading book.

Adverbs

Adverbs tell us more about **verbs**.
Adverbs often end in **ly**.

Alan **excitedly** opened his presents.

Adverbs tell us how, when or where something happens or is done.

1 Look carefully at the sentences. Circle the adverb in each one.

She gently placed the eggs in the basket.

Kylie sang beautifully.

Always look carefully before you cross the road.

We quietly sat down and waited.

2 Use each of these adverbs in your own sentences.

slowly

_____

angrily

_____

tightly

_____

quickly

_____

This topic deals with adverbs of manner (i.e. that describe how something is done) but there are other types. Adverbs of time tell us when actions take place, e.g. tomorrow, often; adverbs of place tell us where actions take place, e.g. inside, upstairs.

Nouns and verbs 1

The **verbs** in a sentence must match the **nouns**.
If they don't the sentence doesn't make sense.

> The **dog bark** at the cat.   *Doesn't make sense.*
>
> The **dog barks** at the cat.   <u>*Does*</u> *make sense.*

1 Circle the verb in each sentence.

Maddie plays on the swing.

Tyler knocks over the glass.

The children run to the park.

The mouse eats the cheese.

2 Tick (✔) the sentences that make sense.
Cross (✘) the sentences that don't make sense.

I runs to the playground. ☐

Bake the cake for 20 minutes. ☐

Everyone love the film. ☐

Sarah walks to her friend's house. ☐

The dog lick my face. ☐

Write one of the wrong sentences correctly.

_____

It will help your child to understand this topic if they know that a singular subject needs a single verb and a plural subject needs a plural verb.

Nouns and verbs 2

Verbs in a sentence must match the nouns.
If they don't the sentence doesn't make sense.

The **snake slither** over the rock.   *Doesn't make sense.*

The **snake slithers** over the rock.   <u>*Does*</u> *make sense.*

1 Rewrite the sentences so that they make sense.

I can reads my book in bed.

_____

Meg eat her lunch quickly.

_____

Liam clap as the actors return.

_____

2 Use each noun in a sentence.
Make sure your sentence makes sense with the correct verb.
Underline the verb.

dog _____

gate _____

tiger _____

Write some sentences but leave the noun out. Ask your child to correctly add a noun that agrees with the verb in each sentence.

Conjunctions

Two sentences can be joined by adding a word between them. The joining word is called a **conjunction**.

We can use the conjunctions **when**, **if**, **that** or **because** to join sentences.

We left early. I felt ill.
We left early **because** I felt ill.
I will come to your house **if** my Mum says it's OK.
We will have tea **when** Mum comes home.
It was so cold outside **that** my nose turned red.

Conjunctions can tell us **when** or **why** something happens.

1 Copy and join the sentences with a conjunction from the box.

    when   if   that   because

Sasha was very hungry. He had missed breakfast.

_____

He was so tired. He went straight to bed.

_____

They had just left home. It started to rain.

_____

It will be fun at the beach. Sandra comes too.

_____

2 Finish the sentences in your own words.

It was her favourite song because _____

I will finish my homework when _____

You will get ill if _____

Noun phrases

A **phrase** is a group of words that work together in a sentence. In a **noun phrase**, the noun is the main word. The noun phrase tells you about the noun.

The **shiny blue ball** bounced over the wall.

1. Underline the noun phrases in these sentences.

   He was wearing shiny new shoes.

   Sheena is my best friend.

   Mum has made iced fairy cakes for tea.

   Put the empty cups on the table.

2. Write each of these noun phrases in a sentence.

   a little bag

   _____

   the soft, white pillow

   _____

   an exciting story

   _____

Ask your child to think of some familiar nouns. Encourage them to come up with adjectives (see page 19) for the nouns to make noun phrases that tell you more about the nouns.

Exclamation marks

This is an **exclamation mark** !
It can be used at the end of a sentence
to show shock, surprise, upset or a command.

It's not fair!

1 Copy and add an exclamation mark to the sentences.

Watch out _____

Stop, thief _____

Quick, we have to hurry _____

This dead mouse stinks _____

Wow, look at that _____

2 Add a full stop, question mark or exclamation mark to these sentences.

Where is my hat_____

Ben likes running_____

I don't believe it_____

What time is it_____

Be quiet, everyone_____

Highlight to your child that an exclamation mark is made with a full stop, so it comes at the end of a sentence.

Apostrophes 2

An apostrophe can show when something belongs to someone.

One owner = noun + **'s**	Kate**'s** dog
More than one owner, with noun ending in s = noun +**'**	The girls**'** dog

1 These are all singular nouns.
Copy the phrase and add the missing apostrophe.

the builders hat   _____

the horses hoof   _____

the boys coat   _____

the climbers rope   _____

2 These are all plural nouns.
Copy the phrase and add the missing apostrophe.

the animals food   _____

the boys football match   _____

the teachers books   _____

the sharks teeth   _____

This is a tricky topic for children to grasp. Work through the rules on this page with your child and discourage your child from adding apostrophes anywhere but where they know they are needed.

Verbs – past tense

A **verb** is usually a doing word.

Andy **walks** to school.

Some verbs tell us what has *already happened*.

Andy **walked** to school.

The **verb** is in the **past tense**.

Sometimes we talk about an action in the past that *continued to happen*.

Andy **was walking** to school.

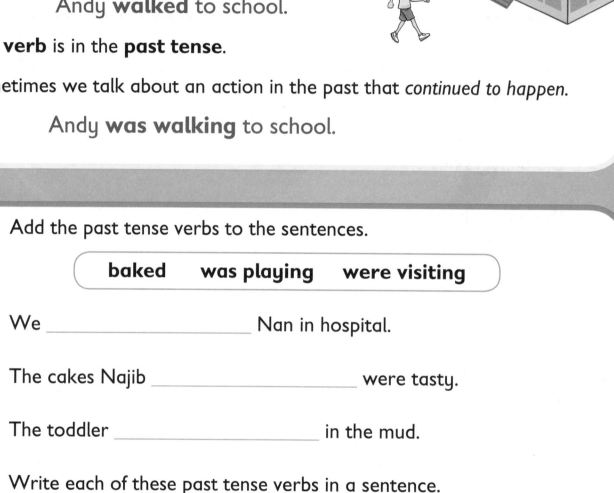

1 Add the past tense verbs to the sentences.

| baked | was playing | were visiting |

We _____ Nan in hospital.

The cakes Najib _____ were tasty.

The toddler _____ in the mud.

2 Write each of these past tense verbs in a sentence.

were looking _____

heard _____

was hoping _____

Give your child some short sentences written in the present, e.g. I brush my teeth, I am watching television. Ask them to write each of the sentences in the past tense, e.g. I brushed my teeth, I was watching television.

Writing sentences 3

Sentences can be **statements, commands, questions** or **exclamations**.
Statements tell you something and end with a **full stop** (.) I can swim.
Commands tell you to do something and end with a **full stop** (.) Sit down.
Exclamations can show excitement and end with an **exclamation mark** (!) That's great!
Questions ask you something and end with a **question mark** (?)
How are you?

1 Read the passage. Copy down three sentences, one that is a question, one that is a statement and one that is an exclamation.

"When will we get there?" asked Tom. He was very tired after waking up early.
"Not long now," Mum replied.
Then everything went wrong.
"Look out, there is a cat in the road!" shouted Tom.
The car skidded to a stop, just missing the cat...

_____

_____

_____

2 Write a sentence that is:

a statement _____

a command _____

an exclamation _____

a question _____

As extra practice, write some sentences that should end with full stops, question marks and exclamation marks. Ask your child to add the missing punctuation marks.

How am I doing?

1 Write the **plural** of each of the nouns.

bee _____ fox _____

witch _____ spoon _____

banana _____ vest _____

2 Join the short sentences with **and**, **but** or **or**.

Tim played football. He scored a goal.

_____

Zoe ran up the road. She missed the bus.

_____

Would you like chips for tea? Would you like mash for tea?

_____

Kyle forgot his bag. It didn't matter.

_____

3 Write four **past tense verbs**.
Remember the past tense is when something has already happened.

_____ _____

_____ _____

4 Fill each gap with a **verb**.

The children _____ a story.

Aimee _____ her flute.

Daniel _____ his breakfast.

Mr Morris _____ at the dog.

5 Copy the **proper nouns** correctly.

new york   **jumper**   austria   sandwich

zoo   **meena**   **september**   computer

_____   _____

_____   _____

6 Write these sentences correctly.
Remember capital letters, full stops, commas, question marks and exclamation marks.

we have run out of time

_____

when can I cook tea

_____

I need to go to tetbury to buy milk eggs butter and bread

_____

Go back to the topics that your child still finds tricky.

Answers

Capital letters
Page 4

1 A B **C** D E F **G** H I J K **L** M N O **P** Q R **S** T U V W **X** Y Z

2 It is a hot day.

The dog sat on a cat.

We like sweets.

Full stops
Page 5

1 The pool is fun.

A girl plays tennis.

Dan walks to school.

The hen laid an egg.

2 Child to complete sentences ending with a full stop.

Nouns
Page 6

1 boat, tree, chair, dog, ring, sun

2 Child to list nouns s/he can see around them.

Proper nouns 1
Page 7

1 The following words circled:

Meena, London, Ben, Africa, Cinderella, Tonkin Road, Mr Atkin, France

2 Child's answers to questions using proper nouns i.e. place names and people starting with capital letters.

Capital letters and full stops
Page 8

1 It is raining.

We like playing games.

Sam is swimming.

2 Child's own sentences, correctly punctuated, with capital letter and full stop using the following words:

Friday, swimming, school

lion, sleep, tree

sweets, shop, buy

Writing sentences 1
Page 9

1 The ice feels cold.

Dan forgot his book.

The shop sells sweets.

2 Cats sleep anywhere.

Children splash in the puddles. /
The children splash in puddles.

The car is grey.

Verbs
Page 10

1 eating, cycling, laughing, skiing, slipping, standing

2 Child's own sentences using verbs from ①.

Questions
Page 11

1 Where are you going?

Why is your coat muddy?

When can I eat my snack?

What is his name?

2 e.g. What is the weather like?

e.g. What time do I need to get up?

e.g. Who is your best friend?

Writing sentences 2
Page 12

1 The sun feels hot.

The dog jumped in the river.

Keith enjoys ice cream.

Anna lost her bag.

2 e.g. We are going on holiday.

e.g. The teacher is grumpy.

e.g. The lion bites the zookeeper.

Commas in lists
Page 13

1 In a car you find keys, maps, seats and seatbelts.

In a house you find doors, windows, beds, tables and chairs.

In a wardrobe you find coats, shirts, trousers, dresses and shoes.

In a shed you find pots, seeds, spades, forks and rakes.

2 Things you find at a school: teachers, water, books, displays, children

Things you find at a swimming pool: floats, towels, water, goggles, till, children

Things you find at a post office: packages, till, postmaster, children, stamps, displays

Singular and plural
Page 14

1 spider spiders

owl owls

chip chips

man men

dish dishes

kiss kisses

beach beaches

Proper nouns 2
Page 15

1 We love walking Barney on Exmoor.

Alex Roberts was late for school on Monday.

Italy is further away than France.

2 Mr James Royman

61 Carpenter Road

Crouch End

London

United Kingdom

How am I doing?
Page 16

1

Nouns	Proper nouns	Verbs
towel	Thursday	run
newspaper	Wales	kick
kite	Ben	write
lion	Cinderella	dance

2 March comes before April.

What time shall we meet?

Don't forget to bring sweets, crisps and apples.

Can Tom come to Baker Park too?

Joining sentences 1
Page 17

1 The leaves fell off the tree and they were raked into a pile.

Zack forgot his coat but he didn't forget his school bag.

The bird caught a worm and it took the worm back to its nest.

2 Child's own sentence endings.

Apostrophes 1
Page 18

1 hasn't

they're

couldn't

I'll

2 We're having a great holiday.
I can't wait to go swimming tonight.
Lucy says she'll be back soon.
Harry didn't come to school today.

32